BUNGALOW BASICS
BEDROOMS

By Paul Duchscherer
Photography by Douglas Keister

Pomegranate
SAN FRANCISCO

Published by Pomegranate Communications, Inc.
Box 6099, Rohnert Park, California 94927
800-227-1428; www.pomegranate.com

Pomegranate Europe Ltd.
Unit 1, Heathcote Business Centre, Hurlbutt Road
Warwick, Warwickshire CV34 6TD, U. K.

Library of Congress Cataloging-in-Publication Data
Duchscherer, Paul.
   Bungalow basics. Bedrooms / text by Paul Duchscherer ; photographs by
Douglas Keister.
     p. cm.
   ISBN 0-7649-2214-9
   1. Bungalows–United States. 2. Bedrooms–United States. 3. Arts and crafts
movement–United States. I. Title: Bedrooms. II. Keister, Douglas. III. Title.

  NA7571 .D82 2003
  728'.373'0973–dc21

                        2002030705
Pomegranate Catalog No. A659

Designed by Patrice Morris

Printed in Korea

12 11 10 09 08 07 06 05 04 03   10 9 8 7 6 5 4 3 2 1

This book is dedicated to the discovery,
appreciation, and preservation of bungalows,
and especially to all those who
love and care for them.

Acknowledgments

Because of space limitations, we regret that it is not possible to acknowledge each of those individuals and organizations who have helped us with this book. Our heartfelt appreciation is extended especially to all the homeowners who, by graciously sharing their homes with us, have made this book a reality. Special thanks are given also to Sandy Schweitzer, John Freed, and Don Merrill for their tireless support, unflagging encouragement, and invaluable assistance. We salute you!

Space constraints also preclude us from listing every credit due to each deserving and talented artisan, architect, designer, craftsperson, and manufacturer whose work appears in this book. We offer them our deepest gratitude for the opportunity to include it here. Alternatively, our readers may wish to consult the extensive credit listings in our earlier book series, published by Penguin Putnam Inc. (comprising *The Bungalow: America's Arts & Crafts Home, Inside the Bungalow: America's Arts & Crafts Interior,* and *Outside the Bungalow: America's Arts & Crafts Garden*), which make reference to many of the images that are also included in this book.

P rivacy in small houses is a luxury. Bungalow bedrooms, even if small, were prized as places to escape from the rest of the household. The reality of bungalow living was that sometimes rooms, including bedrooms, had to be used for varying activities at different times of day. Larger families might have had to convert their living and dining rooms into extra sleeping space. The opportunities for personal privacy increased if the house had a den or perhaps a third bedroom. Attics also offered potential private space.

Bedrooms were usually allotted space for the minimum furnishings: bed, nightstand, and dresser. Bungalow plans tended to give the lion's share of space (sometimes half the square footage) to the public rooms (living and dining). The remaining space was divided between the private (bed) and the utilitarian (kitchen and bath) rooms. In bungalows, unlike contemporary houses, the private and utilitarian rooms were usually of modest proportions.

This allocation of space according to function (public, utilitarian, and private) turned out to be a successful solution for small houses in the past. Today, the prospect of living in bedrooms of minimal size can send occupants accustomed to more space scurrying to remodel.

Bedrooms in a bungalow were typically positioned off a short hallway, usually with a bathroom sandwiched between them. The hallway, often leading from the dining room, created a transition and separation from the main living areas. It was common for at least one bedroom to have doors on two sides, to allow flexible access. Bungalows were known for their convenience, and both bedrooms might have direct access to the bathroom. Some bedrooms were also fitted with sinks (see Figures 8 and 9).

Light, and especially air circulation, were major planning considerations. Bungalow bedrooms were most likely to be located at corners, where windows could be placed on two walls. When the bedroom had a middle wall location, a double (or possibly triple) window might have had to suffice. Some bedrooms were blessed with a bay window, almost invariably spanned below with a built-in window seat, which lifted up to give access to storage inside (Figures 11, 19, 30, and 47).

Closets are a requirement of all bedrooms, but in bungalows their size varied widely. Better-planned houses had fairly generous (sometimes even walk-in) closets close to the requirements of today's home construction. Many early-twentieth-century closets had small openable windows so that clothing could be aired. Often a built-in arrangement of drawers or open shelves in closets reduced the need for more bedroom furniture. Some closets were augmented by built-in dresser drawers and storage cabinets that faced directly into the bedroom (Figures 9 and 10). When rooms without closets, such as dens, needed to be used as temporary bedrooms, a freestanding wardrobe or armoire was the likely solution.

While not typical, a desirable feature for bungalow bedrooms was a door opening directly to the outdoors, especially if the bedroom adjoined an inviting garden or outside sitting area, as in Figures 15 and 17. Many homeowners seeking a minimally invasive remodel have found adding such a door rewarding (Figure 20). For bedrooms on the second floor, a balcony was a desirable feature. Balconies might have adjoined windows in a dormer or gable or perhaps been notched into the roofline (Figures 3, 5, and 19).

Most families grow, and it could be challenging to create enough sleeping space for everyone. Any extra or convertible space (a den or a breakfast room, for example) was likely to be appropriated as an additional bedroom or children's playroom. The early twentieth century was a time when much attention was given in design periodicals and books to creating home environments that would encourage children to engage in constructive play and develop learning skills. A nursery featured in *The Craftsman* magazine in 1905 proposed board-and-batten walls with a blackboard installed between the battens, so that the children could be free to draw in chalk.

Vintage decorating magazines are good sources for bungalow-related ideas (Figures 33 and 35) and contain abundant advertisements of bedroom and nursery-related furnishings (Figure 36). Wall covering lines included charming children's patterns and borders that could be combined in whimsical applications (Figures 38 and 39).

Even if the attic was unfinished, many bungalows had stairways built in from the start. The next best thing was having a floorplan that anticipated a future staircase. This feature, making possible more bedroom space upstairs when necessary, was attractive to homebuyers. Accessible unfinished attic spaces had other potential uses as well. Many became children's playrooms. In some locations, bungalows were constructed with full or partial basements, which might allow space for additional children's bedrooms or indoor play areas.

Another bedroom-related use for attic spaces was to incorporate a sleeping porch, which might be used only seasonally (Figure 25). In the early twentieth century, many Americans believed that sleeping in an open, unheated space and breathing lots of fresh air were deterrents to dangerous respiratory diseases. Usually fitted with as many windows as possible, attic sleeping porches might be located across the end of a gable, sometimes adjoining an upstairs bedroom, as shown in Figures 26 and 28 to 30. Although milder climates allowed year-round use, sleeping porches in most parts of the country were enclosed by glass storm windows during the winter months. Despite their solid roofs, sleeping porches were considered outdoor spaces and needed floor, wall, and ceiling finishes that could withstand damp, cold, windy weather. Beadboard (tongue-and-groove) paneling was used for the walls and ceilings of many sleeping porches (Figures 27 and 28). Its narrow, tightly fitted wooden slats were either painted or stained and varnished. In some houses, other durable exterior surfaces, such as wood siding or shingles, were used (Figure 30). The flooring was usually a softwood (like fir), covered with porch-floor paint or varnished. Overlays of linoleum, oilcloth, or even grass matting were added for pattern and texture. Sometimes a heavy canvaslike material was glued onto the entire floor and painted with enamel to repel moisture.

The typical sleeping porch was sparsely furnished—a single bed or two (Figure 26), sometimes only folding cots that were also used for camping. When sleeping porches were located on a bungalow's first floor, they were almost always directly off a bedroom (and sometimes accessible from more than one). If the family insisted on having a sleeping porch and no other option existed, the front porch might be screened in and used as one. Because space was at a premium in bungalows, the fate of many sleeping porches was eventual conversion to finished and heated spaces dedicated to other purposes (Figure 33). If convenient to plumb, sleeping porches might be converted to laundry rooms or extra bathrooms. In a compact house like a bungalow, any "stray" space was unlikely to last long before it was tagged for another purpose to suit the family's needs.

Particularly ingenious built-ins were concocted to create extra sleeping space. Developed and used throughout the years of bungalow popularity were built-in "disappearing beds." Most of these were variations of the so-called Murphy bed (named for its inventor and early manufacturer), essentially a wall-mounted compartment that stored a bed in a space-saving vertical position (Figure 12). Pulled down when needed, a Murphy bed had a mattress secured to a hinged metal frame. When closed, the bed was concealed by a door (or hinged panel attached to its underside) and, more importantly, left the floor space clear. Some bungalow dens featured Murphy beds, which allowed quick and convenient conversion to guestrooms. The smallest bungalow floor plans actually lacked a bedroom and thus were the likeliest candidates for disappearing beds. These beds were also very popular in the tight quarters of single-room apartments of the early 1900s.

Concepts for the disappearing bed were routinely proposed and frequently patented. Most consisted of a pullout, foldout, flip-down, or rollout arrangement (Figures 13 and 14), to expose a mattress housed in an innocent-looking wooden cabinet masquerading as a dining room sideboard, a living room desk, a storage cabinet, or an armoire (Figure 38). Since these pieces tended to be cumbersome to use and maintain (or move), relatively few of the earliest examples survive. Perhaps the most inventive early-twentieth-century example of a patented concealed bed was one that converted from an apparent built-in high-backed bench into a screened-in bed-sized sleeping porch, as in Figures 31 and 32.

Homeowners adding a master bedroom to a bungalow often find

the attic level the most promising (and least invasive) place. It might also have space for another bathroom, a far greater amount of closet space than elsewhere, and a sitting area or study. Major remodels of attics are not to be undertaken lightly, as they often demand extensive reframing of the roof and floor structures, plus the insertion of windows or skylights for light and ventilation. If windows, dormers, or skylights are added, great care should be taken to avoid compromising the form of the original roof and the style of the house (Figures 19 and 30). Changes to original bedrooms can, however, be among the least obtrusive of room modifications in a bungalow, because significant intact period features that might be destroyed by remodeling are far more likely to be found in the public spaces.

With practicality and maintenance in mind, original bungalow designers selected easily cleaned, "hygienic" surfaces for bungalow floors and walls. Often recommended for bedroom floors was wood, usually stained but sometimes painted. Linoleum and area rugs were popular ways to introduce color and pattern, and they were preferred to fitted (wall-to-wall) carpets because they could be washed and thus reduce dust (Figure 35).

Woodwork finishes often (but not always) varied from private to public areas. Popularly perceived as more hygienic, white or cream-colored enamel was the choice most commonly suggested for bed-room woodwork (Figures 1, 2, and 4 to 8) and was likely to extend into the adjacent hall, bathroom, and kitchen. For bungalow living and dining rooms (and dens), deeper, richer color schemes set off by darkly stained woodwork were most fashionable. If the occupants preferred, the dark woodwork of the front rooms might be carried into the bedrooms and perhaps throughout the house (Figures 3, 10, 16, 21, 22, and 24). Debate over color schemes was avoided in some early bungalows (especially those used as vacation homes) by paneling walls and ceiling completely in wood (Figures 9, 11, 19, 30, and 34).

If the bedroom woodwork was painted a shade of white, what wall colors were considered appropriate? As well documented in paint catalogs of the period, the most recommended bedroom colors were the softest shades of golden yellow, pale green, blue or blue-green, lavender-gray, or grayish rose (Figures 1, 2, 33, and 36). Considered even better if done by the homeowner, hand stenciling (on woodwork, walls, or textiles) accorded with the Arts and Crafts concept of including handicrafts in home decoration (Figures 41 to 45). Other craft work was routinely encouraged as well, especially in textiles (curtains, pillows, and table linens), which could display an owner's appliqué or embroidery skills, as shown in Figures 3, 7, 47, 49, and 51.

Wallpaper had long been a popular choice for decorating schemes, with few rivals in sheer variety of effects and long-lasting impact. Although it might be found in any room, wallpaper was especially common in bedrooms. Manufacturers offered inexpensive, color-coordinated sets of papers, in which an overall pattern could be combined with a wide frieze or narrow border and a simple ceiling paper (often printed with a light-reflecting "mica" ink). Large floral patterns (Figure 47) and leafy tapestry-style designs (Figure 45) were the most popular early-twentieth-century choices for bedroom wallpaper. Some were adaptations of eighteenth-century colonial-era patterns. Tailored stripes were a tasteful alternative to complex florals (Figure 49). Otherwise plain papers (called "oatmeal papers") relied on their texture for interest and were the background of many patterns (Figure 38). Other textured papers imitated linen, grass cloth, or burlap. Some bedroom wall coverings were actual textiles, but in most households these were more likely to be considered for the public rooms because most textile coverings cost more than paper.

Furniture for bungalow bedrooms tended to take a back seat to living and dining room furnishings, which commanded more attention and a greater budget. In fact, some design advice books suggested that the least expensive furniture update was simply to paint existing bedroom furniture with white enamel to match the room's woodwork, as in Figures 1 and 2. Just as bungalow owners today collect Arts and Crafts pieces for every room, during the bungalow's heyday, choices for bedroom furniture might have included Craftsman period pieces, although they were not as pervasive as might be imagined. Instead, for bedrooms and most other rooms (especially in the

1920s), Colonial Revival was the most popular furniture style in America (Figures 35, 42, and 45). Displayed in every department store and widely advertised in decorating periodicals, matching multiple-piece bedroom sets (or so-called suites) were the favorite choice of typical middle-class families.

Because bedrooms had as much privacy as bungalow spaces could offer, they allowed greater freedom of expression in decorating than most other rooms. Whether a bedroom was a repository of fashionable new taste or a mishmash of leftovers, its greatest appeal was its seclusion and sense of peace. A timeless feeling of comfort and security arose from closing its door on the world, retreating into a private sanctuary, and gaining a renewed perspective on life. 🐛

BUNGALOW BASICS

❦ 1 & 2. These two bedroom designs appeared in the 1910 book *Your Home and Its Decoration,* published by the Sherwin-Williams Paint Company. The room in Figure 1 (top illustration) has the typical pale color palette recommended for bungalow bedrooms by various periodicals and design advice books of the day. The stylized floral motifs in the stenciled frieze, in softly pleasing contrast with the white woodwork and the subtle yellow-green walls, echo the colors of the rug. In Figure 2, the color scheme (again borrowed from the rug) is brighter, using yellow-orange walls that work equally well with white woodwork. Showing how a narrow border might be positioned in a wide frieze area, the floral stencil design repeats the deep green in the rug. Sherwin-Williams may have used these illustrations to encourage use of white paint for furniture.

Archival images from the collection of Timothy Hansen and Dianne Ayres,
Arts & Crafts Period Textiles

🐚 3. On the second floor of a Craftsman-style bungalow, this unusually roomy 1908 bedroom retains its original lighting and darkly stained fir woodwork. A pair of windows and the doors leading to a small balcony were recently fitted with curtains of a linen and flax blend that have been embroidered in a ginkgo motif adapted from a Gustav Stickley design.

Curtains by Dianne Ayres, Arts & Crafts Period Textiles

4. Typical of attic bedrooms, the ceiling of this 1911 room is angled like the roof. Windows on more than one wall offer better air circulation in bedrooms. Fitted with linen Roman shades, the casement windows have inward-swinging screens. All the furnishings here are by the Roycroft Community and of the period.

🐾 5. While outside doors were not a typical feature in bedrooms, this attic room (in the same house as in Figure 4) has a French door leading onto a narrow balcony. Native American textiles, also admired in the Craftsman period, are much in evidence. Through the windows, the slanting undersides of the roof eaves are visible.

🐝 6. A master bedroom suite with a separate sitting area (not typical of bungalow plans) has been made by combining two adjoining rooms. Centered on a fireplace opposite the bed (out of view), the sitting area features a high wainscot and plate rail, with a William Morris wallpaper design above it. Arts and Crafts period pieces are mixed with interpretations by contemporary artisans (the bed, for example).

Bed by Debey Zito Fine Furniture; wallpaper by Bradbury & Bradbury

🐝 7. In a bedroom of unusually generous size, a cheerful sitting and work area is visible beyond the posts of the footboard. A cream-colored paint scheme and new soft yellow curtains amplify the feeling of lightness. Above the small desk where the curtains are parted, are two Arts and Crafts-style appliquéd designs.

Curtains by Dianne Ayres, Arts & Crafts Period Textiles

🐛 8. This photograph from a 1923 edition of *The Home* shows off the touted convenience of a built-in sink, hidden behind a door alongside a pair of clothes closets. Convenient built-ins were a key part of the bungalow "ideal," but a personal sink separate from the bathroom was not common.

Archival image from the collection of Paul Duchscherer

9. In an early 1899 bedroom with an all-redwood interior, a wall of built-ins features a vintage marble-lined sink area and a closet at the far left behind a matching door. Commodious dresser drawers and a storage cabinet are built in between them.

❧ 10. Next to a bay window in this 1906 bedroom is a conveniently arranged built-in that incorporates a large closet, five dresser drawers, and a cupboard for hats. In modest bedrooms, such built-ins lessened the need for other bulky furniture.

11. Recalling the space-saving ingenuity of ship interiors, this redwood-lined 1899 bedroom features a built-in dresser and cupboard fitted snugly beneath a small open staircase to an attic loft. Unusual storage (under a lift-up hatch) is provided beneath the stair landing. A small clinker brick fireplace offers warmth.

❧ 12. A retractable Murphy bed is part of the built-in storage wall in this 1911 bedroom. Pulled down as needed, the bed is otherwise hidden behind a large framed dressing mirror. Such beds were popular space-savers in rooms for multiple uses.

13 & 14. Installed in a den that could be quickly converted to a bedroom, this clever 1908 "disappearing bed" is disguised as a simple storage unit of drawers with a cupboard and built into a wall below an open bookcase. Such novel space-saving beds were seen in many bungalow plans. This variant moves on rubber rollers.

🐛 15. Like a summer camp cabin in the woods, this all-redwood Craftsman-style guesthouse, which was rebuilt after a fire, can hold lots of company. Besides these two beds, it has a sleeping loft accessible by ladder and a sofa bed (out of view). Stacked towels serve the adjoining bathroom and a spa recessed into the front porch decking.

🐛 16. An unusual corner bay window and a two-level beamed redwood ceiling give this 1905 bedroom special architectural interest. Suspended from the beams, period art-glass pendant lights are highlighted against the wood. An English Arts and Crafts armoire by Liberty of London is among the room's furnishings.

17. Part of a new addition, this bedroom has an all-wood ceiling directly inspired by the one in Figure 16, but it is more Asian in feeling and modified in its proportions to suit this room's smaller scale. Discreet indirect lighting is set on top of the beams that project inward. The wide outside doorway brings nature inside.

Design by John Zanakis, House of Orange

18. Created from salvaged timbers, the angled and beamed ceiling of this 1929 bedroom showcases the builder's art. Adding texture, color, and pattern, the exposed brick walls anchor the ceiling. The small arching alcove with two windows is a projecting dormer, flanked by a pair of closets with peaked doors.

🐾 19. Entirely finished in redwood, this attic bedroom retains all its 1905 features: a soaring ceiling, a cozy fireplace, French door access to an outdoor balcony, a built-in window seat, and open bookshelves. Although the door and the two original casement windows provided good air circulation, a large openable skylight has now been installed.

🐿 20. In a recent renovation, two bedrooms have been combined into a master suite that includes a walk-in closet, dressing room, and large bath. Inspired by Prairie School architecture, the room's sleek lines extend to the custom-built bed and the built-in TV/storage unit at right. Connecting the bedroom with the outdoors are new French doors and a tilt-out window above the bed. Antique lighting is used throughout.

Rug by Blue Hills Studio

🐾 21. In Greene and Greene's 1909 Thorsen House in Berkeley, California (now home to the Sigma Phi Society, a college fraternity), this bedroom and several other rooms were expertly staged with period pieces, re-creating its era as a private residence, during a 1996 summer exhibition to benefit maintenance of the house. This room also boasts fine woodwork, built-in window valances, and a fireplace decorated with Rookwood tiles.

🐾 22. The spacious master bedroom at Greene and Greene's famous 1908 Gamble House in Pasadena, California, shows off the architects' skill and artistry in a handsome fireplace and inviting inglenook, finely detailed woodwork, indirect lighting, and inlaid furniture. Above the built-in bench, an art-glass window opens to the stairwell for inside air circulation.

🐨 23. Adjoining the primary bedrooms, spacious open-air sleeping porches are a key part of the Gamble House. Seen from one of these are another sleeping porch off the master bedroom (at right) and the original garage (now the Gamble House Bookstore). Pasadena's mild climate allowed use of these outdoor spaces year-round.

🐝 24. With its pair of original nickel-plated beds designed by the architects, the guest bedroom at the Gamble House makes visitors want to stay over. Greene and Greene's signature attention to detail extends to every element, including the superb mahogany-and-art-glass wall sconces and the exquisite maple furniture.

❦ 25. Shown in a 1923 edition of *The Home,* this sleeping porch ringed with a pergola illustrates how such a porch could be added to a home. The mania for sleeping porches began in the early 1900s, fueled by the belief that fresh air was an antidote to many respiratory ailments.

❦ 26. An interior view of a 1920s sleeping porch shows typical furnishings: a spartan arrangement of single beds or cots in a compact, window-lined enclosure. The frieze and ceiling areas here are inset with panels of a woven wall covering to create a more finished look.

Archival images from the collection of Paul Duchscherer

27. With walls and ceiling lined in beadboard (tongue-and-groove) paneling, this open-air sleeping porch is a rare survivor from 1906. Never covered by glass or screens, the wall openings still have roller-shade pulleys above, a sign that the shades were drawn up from the bottom for privacy.

🐨 28. This sleeping porch, facing the rear garden of a 1911 bungalow, is one of a matched pair that were original parts of the house; its twin is partly visible at the far left. Fully restored, the casement windows and screens on the three outside walls offer flexible air control.

🐨 29. This 1911 bedroom adjoins an original sleeping porch that has been converted into a small and sunny home office. The deep eaves of the bedroom's sloping roof are visible through the windows at left. Notable Gustav Stickley-designed furnishings include a bed, a Morris chair, and a bookrack.

🐨 30. A sleeping porch at left, incorpo-
rated into the end of a roof gable, con-
nects with this 1905 attic bedroom. The
skylight was added, but the window seat
is original. Unheated areas like this
sleeping porch required wall finishes
such as the wood siding and shingles
used here, which could withstand the
elements.

✿ 31 & 32. What appears to be a high-backed Craftsman-style settle (left) has another identity as a disappearing bed, but with a difference. This rare unit, an example of "patent furniture," is fitted with a simple sliding mechanism resembling a breadbox lid, which can close the bed off from the inside room and open it to a screened-in cutout in the wall, offering the option of slumber in the great outdoors.

Photographs by Paul Duchscherer

🐚 33. This glass-enclosed sunporch, depicted in a 1923 edition of *The Home,* could double as a guestroom or sleeping porch. Although informal, the space is decorated stylishly with wicker furniture and colorful textiles for the curtains, upholstery, pillows, and lampshades.

Archival image from the collection of Paul Duchscherer

❦ 34. Originally enclosed by screens, this 1904 redwood-paneled space was first a sleeping porch and later converted to a heated bedroom. A painter and textile artist, the homeowner adorned the bed with a handmade quilt and decorated its frame with whimsical nature motifs. Hand-carved bears from Japan pose on the bedposts.

🌱 35. A floor covering manufacturer used this bedroom in a 1920s advertisement to show its product in a typical boy's bedroom. Attic bedrooms usually have sloping ceilings and often have dormer windows, which can make brightly lit study areas.

Archival image from the collection of Timothy Hansen and Dianne Ayres, Arts & Crafts Period Textiles

🐾 36. This stylishly outfitted children's room, which appeared in a 1923 edition of *The Home,* took its color scheme from the floral curtain fabric. Closely related colors appear on the floor, the walls, a stenciled animal frieze, and the painted furnishings.

Archival image from the collection of Paul Duchscherer

❧ 37. *(left)* Western and cowboy collectibles make an entertaining display in a cozy attic bedroom. The flat central area of the three-sided ceiling, installed in a large dormer beneath a peaked gable roof, helps make the narrow room feel wider. Moldings used to panel the ceiling add a horizontal feeling.

❧ 38. *(overleaf)* Rare, intact 1920s vintage wallpaper has survived in a child's bedroom. Against a textured "oatmeal paper" background, panels depicting zoo scenes are placed in the frieze, and larger panels of delphiniums are set into the door. A disappearing bed is cleverly concealed in the wood cabinet at right.

🐘 39. The wallpaper designs in this product illustration from the 1916–1917 catalog of James Davis Artistic Paperhangings were proposed for use in children's rooms. Some figures were intended to be cut out and used creatively in découpage.

Archival image from the collection of Paul Duchscherer

🐘 40. Around the perimeter of this child's bedroom, a plate rail allows for display and storage of books and small toys. The wide wallpaper frieze, with paired bunnies set beneath stylized floral motifs, is an adaptation of an Arts and Crafts period pattern.

Wallpaper by Carol Mead Design

🐦 41. In a 1905 house originally built as a summer home, this spacious bedroom was recently given a makeover. Closely related in form to the example in Figure 40, the stenciled frieze adapts a 1905 Harvey Ellis design from *The Craftsman* magazine. British Arts and Crafts influence is also apparent in the period armoire and new carpet.

🐚 42. Popular in the Arts and Crafts era, the pinecone motif reappears in a newly stenciled border that accents the sloping ceiling of an attic bedroom. Windows with appropriately simple curtains backlight an unusual Craftsman-style phonograph.

Stencil by Helen Foster

🐚 43. *(left)* A floral stencil design was re-created from a vintage photograph of this bedroom that showed its wallpaper frieze. The soft colors and delicate scale reflect recommended design ideas of the early twentieth century.

Stencil by Lynne McDaniel

🐚 44. *(left, bottom)* This bedroom's graceful stencil pattern of leaves and flowers shows the stylized nature designs that Arts and Crafts period tastemakers preferred to more realistic depictions.

Stencil by Helen Foster

🐚 45. A 1915 bedroom retains its original decorating scheme at the Lanterman House in La Cañada-Flintridge, California, a house museum near Pasadena. The lush forest motif of the wallpaper is echoed in a stenciled border of stylized oak leaves and acorns set low in the frieze above the picture molding.

🐾 46. A tailored wallpaper frieze, inspired by the decorative work of famed Scottish architect Charles Rennie Mackintosh, incorporates panels with a "Glasgow rose" motif framed by a geometric border. Mackintosh's influence is also seen in the embroidered bedroom curtains made by the owners. The furniture includes both vintage and new Arts and Crafts-style pieces.

Wallpaper by Bradbury & Bradbury

🐝 47. A late-nineteenth-century mainstay of middle-class bedrooms, brass beds like this one with onyx accents remained popular into the twentieth century. An Arts and Crafts period wallpaper pattern of intertwining roses by British designer Walter Crane creates an unusual checkerboard effect. On the bed and window seat are period style pillows.

Wallpaper by Bradbury & Bradbury

🐝 48 & 49. Before and after views of this bungalow bedroom show its makeover from a small, lackluster space with a rather dated 1950s wallpaper mural to one with a sophisticated new treatment inspired by famous Scottish Arts and Crafts architect Charles Rennie Mackintosh. Employing reproduction wallpaper patterns and narrow borders in a soft palette, the new scheme has a linear, architectural quality that fits the room's proportions. A crisp panel arrangement accented with repeating "Glasgow rose" designs unifies the wall and frieze areas. New stenciled textiles for the bedspread, curtains, table cover, and one of the pillows repeat the stylized rose motif.

(right) Wallpaper by Bradbury & Bradbury; textiles by Dianne Ayres, Arts & Crafts Period Textiles

🐾 50 & 51. Before and after views of this typical 1970s-era bedroom show how its plain modern construction with an eight-foot ceiling can be transformed into a new version of Arts and Crafts design with an Asian edge. The poorly placed bathroom door has been rerouted through the adjacent closet at left. Narrow baseboards and door casings have been replaced by wider ones. To create a unifying frieze, moldings connect the tops of the doors and windows. Recycled Japanese shoji panels backed with obscured glass conceal the old aluminum window and security grille. Reproductions of Arts and Crafts pillows and portieres (door curtains popular during the period) combine with old and new furnishings.

(right) Portières and pillows by Dianne Ayres, Arts & Crafts Period Textiles; bed and nightstand by Debey Zito Fine Furniture; painting (above bed) by John Freed.

BUNGALOW BACKGROUND

America's most popular house of the early twentieth century, the bungalow, is making a big comeback as our newest "historic" house. Surviving bungalows are now considered treasures by historic preservationists, while homeowners rediscover the bungalow's appeal as a modest, practical home with a convenient floor plan. This book highlights an important aspect of bungalow interiors.

Webster's New Collegiate Dictionary describes a bungalow as "a dwelling of a type first developed in India, usually one story, with low sweeping lines and a wide verandah." The word *bungalow* derives from the Hindi *bangala,* both an old Hindu kingdom in the Bengal region of India and a rural Bengali hut with a high thatched-roof over-hang creating a covered porch (or verandah) around the perimeter to provide shade from the scorching sun. The height and steep pitch of the roof encouraged the hottest air to rise and escape, while cooler air flowed in at ground level (especially after sundown). The British colonists adapted the design in their own dwellings, and their success spread the concept from India to elsewhere in the British Empire, especially Southeast Asia, Africa, New Zealand, and Australia. By the late eighteenth century, the name *bangala* had been anglicized to *bungalow.*

This name first appeared in print in the United States in 1880. Used in an architectural journal, it described a single-story, shingled Cape Cod summerhouse ringed by covered porches. By the 1900s, *bungalow* had become part of our popular vocabulary, at first associated with vacation homes, both seaside and mountain. The bungalow's informality, a refreshing contrast to stuffy Victorian houses, helped fuel its popularity as a year-round home. It had its greatest fame as a modest middle-class house from 1900 to 1930.

Widely promoted, the bungalow was touted for its modernity, practicality, affordability, convenience, and often-artistic design. Expanding industry and a favorable economy across the country created an urgent need for new, affordable, middle-class housing, which the bungalow was just in time to meet.

In America, a bungalow implied a basic plan, rather than a specific style, of modest house. Typically, it consisted of 1,200 to 1,500 square feet, with living room, dining room, kitchen, two bedrooms, and bathroom all on one level. Some bungalows had roomy attic quarters, but most attics were bare or intended to be developed as the family's needs grew. A bungalow set in a garden fulfilled many Americans' dream of a home of their own.

Widely publicized California bungalows in the early 1900s spawned frenzied construction in booming urban areas across the country. In design, most bungalows built prior to World War I adopted the so-called Craftsman style, sometimes combined with influences from the Orient, the Swiss chalet, or the Prairie style. After the war, public taste shifted toward historic housing styles, and bungalows adapted Colonial Revival, English cottage, Tudor, Mission, and Spanish Colonial Revival features.

Today Craftsman is the style most associated with bungalows. Characterized inside and out by use of simple horizontal lines, Craftsman style relies on the artistry of exposed wood joinery (often visible on front porch detailing). Natural or rustic materials (wood siding, shingles, stone, and clinker brick) are favored. Interiors may be enriched with beamed ceilings, high wainscot paneling, art glass, and hammered copper or metalwork lighting accents.

The word *Craftsman* was coined by prominent furniture manufacturer and tastemaker Gustav Stickley, who used it to label his line of sturdy, slat-backed furniture (also widely known as Mission style), which was influenced by the English Arts and Crafts movement. That movement developed in the mid-nineteenth century as a reaction against the Industrial Revolution. Early leaders such as John Ruskin and William Morris turned to the medieval past for inspiration as they sought to preserve craft skills disappearing in the wake of factory mechanization.

In both the decorative arts (furniture, wallpaper, textiles, glass, metalwork, and ceramics) and architecture, the Arts and Crafts movement advocated use of the finest natural materials to make practical and beautiful designs, executed with skillful handcraftsmanship. One goal was to improve the poor-quality, mass-produced home furnishings available to the rising middle class. Morris and a group of like-minded friends founded a business to produce well-designed, handcrafted goods for domestic interiors. Although the company aspired to make its goods affordable to all, it faced the inevitable conflict between quality and cost. However, its Arts and Crafts example inspired many others in England (and eventually in America) to relearn treasured old craft traditions and continue them for posterity.

As it grew, the movement also became involved in politics, pressing for social reforms. Factory workers trapped in dull, repetitive jobs (with little hope for anything better) were among their chief concerns; they saw the workers' fate as a waste of human potential and talent.

The idealistic and visionary English movement's artistic goals of design reform were more successful than its forays into social reform. Perhaps its greatest success, in both England and the United States, was in giving the public a renewed sense of the value of quality materials, fine craftsmanship, and good design in times of rapid world change.

The Arts and Crafts movement had multiple influences on the

American bungalow. The movement arrived here from England in the early 1900s, just as the bungalow was becoming popular. Among its most successful promoters was Elbert Hubbard, founder of the Roycroft Community, a group of artisans producing handmade books and decorative arts inspired by Morris. Hubbard also published two periodicals and sold goods by mail order.

Gustav Stickley was another American inspired by England's important reform movement and soon was expressing this inspiration in the sometimes austere but well-made designs of his Craftsman style. Becoming an influential promoter of the bungalow as an ideal "Craftsman home," he marketed furniture, lighting, metalwork, and textiles styled appropriately for it. His magazine, *The Craftsman,* was a popular vehicle for his ideas and products, and he sold plans for the Craftsman houses he published in his magazine. The wide popularity of his Craftsman style spread the aesthetic sensibilities of the Arts and Crafts movement into countless American middle-class households, making it a growing influence on architecture and decorative arts here. (England in the early twentieth century remarkably had no middle-class housing form comparable to the American bungalow, but Australia has bungalows of that period, inspired by ours, rather than any from Britain.)

Other manufacturers eventually contributed to Stickley's downfall by blatantly copying his ideas and products and eroding his market share. Once Stickley's exclusive brand name, the word *Craftsman* was assimilated into general use and became public property after his bankruptcy in 1916.

Americans choosing the Craftsman style for their homes, interiors, and furnishings rarely were committed to the artistic and philosophical reforms of the Arts and Crafts movement; most were simply following a vogue. Prospective homeowners (and real estate developers) usually selected their bungalow designs from inexpensive sets of plans marketed in catalogs called plan books; few used an architect's services. Some people even bought prefabricated "ready-cut" or "kit" houses. First sold in 1909 by Sears, Roebuck and Company, prefabricated houses soon were widely copied. In the heat of bungalow mania, Sears and others offered tempting incentives to prospective bungalow buyers, such as bonus financing for their lots. For a time, it was said that if you had a job, you could afford a bungalow. But when jobs were in short supply as the Great Depression hit, many defaulted on their little dream homes, leaving their creditors stung.

The depression ended the heyday of the bungalow, but its practical innovations reappeared in later houses, then more likely to be called cottages. The post-World War II ranch house could be considered the legacy of the bungalow. Only recently has a rising demand for lower-cost houses triggered a reevaluation of vintage bungalow stock as viable housing. In response to public demand, the home planning and construction industries have reprised some of the obvious charms of the bungalow in new homes. A real boon for homeowners seeking to restore or renovate a vintage bungalow (or perhaps build a new one) is today's flourishing Arts and Crafts revival, fueled by the demand for a wide array of newly crafted home furnishings that reflect the traditions and spirit of the Arts and Crafts movement.